St. Raphael's Guidance for Finding Your Soulmate

Written By Saul Cross

This book is reverently dedicated to the Blessed Virgin Mary, our divine advocate and mother. Through her tender intercession, we earnestly seek the guidance of St. Raphael for all those questing to find their soulmate. May the Virgin Mary's pure and compassionate heart strengthen the prayers of St. Raphael within this tome, leading souls to the love and unity that reflect her Son, Jesus Christ. Amen.

St. Raphael's Guidance for Finding Your Soulmate

This book be-
longs to...

. . . .

Thank You!

Honored Reader,

My heartfelt gratitude extends to you for welcoming "St. Raphael's Guidance for Finding Your Soulmate" into your life's journey. Your engagement is a profound source of encouragement, and it's my sincerest wish that the pages of this tome resonate and enrich your spirit.

It is with great pleasure that I invite you to explore the additional dimensions of this work. By scanning the QR code provided, you gain access to an auditory experience of the book's prayers. This element allows you to immerse yourself in their resonant beauty, whether amid your travels, periods of reflection, or in times of calm repose. Beyond the prayers, the QR code also serves as your gateway to an array of carefully curated tools, intended to bolster your quest for spiritual growth.

Your companionship on this path is profoundly valued. May the insights and tenderness shared by Saint Raphael infuse your existence with serenity, reverence, and a celestial connection.

Index

A Note From the Author

Dear reader,

As you embark on this sacred journey through the pages of "St. Raphael's Guidance for Finding Your Soulmate," allow me to take a moment of reflection with you. From the depths of my heart, I, Saul Cross, wish to extend my warmest thoughts and prayers to you, my fellow seeker of divine love and companionship. This book is born out of a profound belief in the power of prayer and the unwavering hope that every soul can discover its counterpart through grace and guidance.

In our current era, where the quest for genuine connection can often seem daunting, it is essential to remember that you are not alone in your search. The Lord, in His infinite mercy, has appointed St. Raphael, the angel of happy encounters, to assist us as we navigate the turbulent waters of modern courtship. The pages that follow are delicately woven with prayers inspired by the lives of saints, the traditions of our Church, and my own spiritual experiences.

Each prayer has been composed with the intention to kindle within you the virtues of faith, hope, and charity—virtues that will illuminate your path as you seek not just a partner, but a soulmate with whom to journey towards Heaven. It is through these holy invocations that we aim to prepare your heart as well as that of your future spouse, crafting a relationship grounded in the sacredness of God's love.

St. Raphael's intercession is a treasure that the Church venerates, particularly when it comes to matters of the heart. His presence in the Book of Tobit gives us a model of faithful stewardship in love—one that we ought to emulate. By offering our supplications through this archangel, we trust that he will guide our steps, ensuring that our relationships are formed, cherished, and preserved in sanctity.

May this novena, and the accompanying array of prayers, serve as faithful companions in your everyday moments of solitude and contemplation. As you recite them, picture St. Raphael presenting your petitions before the throne of God, intertwined with the same holy intention that brought together Tobiah and Sarah in a union of purposeful and prayerful love.

Time and patience are essential ingredients in this spiritual voyage. Do not be disheartened by moments of doubt or prolonged periods of waiting, for the divine timeline is both perfect and mysterious in its unfolding. Take solace in the certainty that the Creator, who knows the deepest desires of your heart, has set a plan in motion that will culminate in a future filled with hope.

In closing, my dear reader, let us journey together, hand in hand, with St. Raphael as our unwavering guide. May your prayerful appeals reach the heavens and align you with the divine will, leading you to the one whose soul resonates harmoniously with your own. Until that blessed encounter, keep steadfast in faith, hope, and love.

In His loving service and yours,

Saul Cross

St. Raphael

In a time when the heavens were as near to the earth as hope is to the human heart, there lived an angel of exceptional grace and kindness, known in the sacred texts and throughout the realms of glory as Raphael. God, in His infinite wisdom, had created Raphael not only as a messenger but as a healer, a guide, and a companion to all who sought divine assistance on their earthly journeys.

Raphael, whose name means "God heals," was renowned among the celestial hosts for his gentle demeanor and his steadfast dedication to the Almighty's work. His presence was like a soft but radiant light, comforting those in distress and instilling courage in the hearts of the weary.

Now, it is told in the sacred annals of the Book of Tobit that a young man named Tobiah was beset by difficulties and this narrative, sweetened by divine love, will illuminate the beautiful role Raphael played in human lives.

Tobiah, obedient and full of faith, found himself on a journey fraught with uncertainty. He needed guidance, for more than just the road he was to travel; his heart was seeking a life companion, a soulmate, a love blessed by the heavens. It was within this tender longing that Raphael, following the will of the Lord, descended to earth, donning the guise of a man. He came to Tobiah as Azariah, a wise and knowing companion, for the Lord loves to work through His creation inspiring them to acts of goodness and virtue.

Together, Tobiah and the incognito Raphael ventured forth, and in their travels, Raphael's guidance proved true and his loyalty unwavering. Hidden from mortal eyes was the splendor of his angelic nature, yet his actions and wisdom betrayed the heavenly grace from which he so humbly originated.

It was not just journey's success that Raphael secured but also the healing of Tobiah's future bride, Sarah, who had suffered greatly before their meeting. Seven times she had known the sorrow of loss, for an evil spirit had preyed upon her happiness. But where others saw insurmountable odds, Raphael saw the opportunity for God's mercy to manifest. In the shadow of prayer and faith, and through Raphael's intercession, the spirit was vanquished, and the path was cleared for the chaste and loving union between Tobiah and Sarah.

The love between these two young souls was pure and illuminated by God's own light; they came together in a marriage that stood as a testament to steadfast prayer, unwavering devotion, and the trust in divine providence. Raphael had not only guided Tobiah through the physical landscape but through the landscape of his own heart to find a love as resolute and as destined as the stars.

Upon completing the heavenly mission, Raphael revealed his true form to Tobiah and his family, humbling those who witnessed the majesty of the divine and bringing them to their knees in awe. The angel who walked as a man reminded them that it was their faith and sincere supplications that called him to their side, just as it is for all who seek aid and comfort in their quest for companionship.

And so, as the angel returned to the celestial sphere, his legacy remained aglow in the love story of Tobiah and Sarah, a guiding light for all young lovers who seek a counterpart to fulfill God's plan for them. Saint Raphael, the serene and joyful healer, continues to be the patron of those yearning for a godly bond, serving as a heavenly beacon for the hearts searching for one another, uniting them under the gaze of the Lord, as he once did for Tobiah and Sarah.

In this light, the prayer to St. Raphael extends beyond mere words; it is an act of trust in the God who heals, who guides, and who brings together souls meant to reflect the sanctity and joy of love sanctified. Let us, therefore, call upon St. Raphael with confidence, knowing that in the divine plan, there is a moment of meeting written in the stars, and an angel ready to guide us there.

"AND NOW THESE THREE
REMAIN: FAITH, HOPE AND
LOVE. BUT THE GREATEST
OF THESE IS LOVE."

- 1 CORINTHIANS 13:13

Intercessory Prayers

In the sacred quest for companionship and the longing of our hearts for a soulmate, we turn to St. Raphael the Archangel, patron of those seeking a life partner. In this journey, it is easy to grow weary, to falter in faith, and to be led astray by the fleeting promises of the world. Yet, it is in this very search that we are called to lean more deeply into the mysteries of divine providence and love. The following 25 prayers are intended to be beacons of light on the path toward holy matrimony. They draw on the wisdom of Scripture and the Church's rich tradition to guide you in praying with intention, focus, and a spirit of surrender to God's perfect timing.

Each prayer addresses different facets of the soulmate-seeking journey: from the longing of the heart to the patience required in waiting, from discerning true love to healing past wounds. By seeking the intercession of St. Raphael, we invite his guidance and company as a friend who led Tobias to Sarah in the Book of Tobit. May these prayers strengthen you, bring clarity to your desires, and align your heart with God's plan. We embark on this novena and the accompanying prayers with the assurance that our pleas are heard, and with faith that in God's time, St. Raphael will guide us to the love for which our hearts were made.

Thank you Lord for...

_____
_____
_____
_____
_____
_____
_____
_____
_____
_____

St. Raphael, intercede for me on...

_____
_____
_____
_____
_____
_____
_____
_____
_____
_____

Intercede for my loved ones...

_____
_____
_____
_____
_____
_____
_____
_____
_____
_____

My Personal Prayer

Trust in God's Plan - Reflecting on Proverbs 3:5-6

O Blessed St. Raphael, faithful servant and friend of those who seek companionship, I come before you seeking your intercession. As the healer and guide for those on life's journey, I ask you to present my humble petition before God, trusting in His divine plan for my life.

Heavenly Father, You have commanded us through Proverbs to "Trust in the Lord with all your heart and lean not on your own understanding; in all your ways submit to him, and he will make your paths straight." With this wisdom nestled in my heart, I pray for the grace to rely on Your profound knowledge and perfect timing in all things, especially in the journey towards finding my soulmate.

As Abraham trusted in You, Lord, when called to leave all that was familiar and embark on the unknown, may I also possess the faith to follow Your will, without demanding signs or assurances. Just as he was ready to sacrifice his son Isaac, guided solely by his reliance on Your promises, let me surrender my anxieties and expectations, trusting that You, who are Love itself, will lead me to the love I am meant to find.

St. Raphael, guide of lovers, help me to discern God's plan for my life with patience and peace. Encourage my heart to remain open to the lessons of love He desires to teach me. May your gentle intercession lead me to a love that reflects the love God has for each of His children.

May the Light of God's truth illuminate my path, and may I be steadfast in my commitment to His guidance. I trust in God's plan for my life, believing in the goodness He has in store for me. Help me, dear St. Raphael, to not grow weary or discouraged but to remain hopeful and joyful in the expectation of

God's blessings.

I entrust my heart's desires to You, knowing that in God's perfect time and divine will, the longings of my heart will be fulfilled. Through your intercession, St. Raphael, may I come to love and be loved in a way that brings glory to God and sanctity to my life.

Amen.

Patience in Waiting - Inspired by Psalm 27:14

O patient St. Raphael, whose healing touch restored sight and brought together destined souls,

I come before you seeking serenity in my heart's long quest.

In the throes of waiting, when impatience unfolds,

May I embrace the grace of patience to cradle my restless spirit.

When shadows of doubt cloud my hopeful gaze,

Let the light of endurance illuminate my path.

Where anxiety seeks to tighten its grip around my dreams,

Grant me the tranquility to breathe deeply the air of perseverance.

As I wait for the appointed time, in the stillness of anticipation,

Teach me to cherish each moment, for in it wisdom gently whispers.

When solitude whispers the fear of unending aloneness,

May the whisper transform into a song of self-discovery and peace.

In the silent corners of my soul, where longing and desire are intertwined,

Remind me that love, true and divine, is worth the journey's weight in time.

For every tear shed in solitude's embrace,

May there bloom a blossom of hope, fragrant with the promise of tomorrow.

Through your intercession, St. Raphael, broker of divine providence,

Impart to me the courage to face the morrow with a steadfast heart.

As I give my trust, so shall I receive assurance;

As I forgive time its slow passage, may time bestow upon me its timely gift.

In quietude and through the tempest of emotions,

Lead me to the sanctuary of acceptance, where patience is both my guard and guide.

With every beat of my expectant heart,

Bind me to the virtue that stands firm when all else is in flux.

St. Raphael, guide my wayward spirit to the harbor of heavenly timing,

For in the symphony of God's perfect plan,

My soulmate, like a hidden melody, awaits the conductor's cue.

Amen.

Discernment in Love - Based on Philippians 1:9-10

O Blessed St. Raphael, Patron of Love and Courtship, we raise our hearts to you in earnest supplication, seeking your powerful intercession in the delicate matter of discernment in love, enlightened by the wisdom that echoes through Philippians 1:9-10. Guide our emotions and our understanding, we pray, so that our love may flourish in knowledge and depth of insight.

As the Lord appeared to Solomon in dreams, granting him the precious gifts of a discerning heart and unmatched wisdom, we humbly implore your assistance, St. Raphael, that we, too, may receive the grace to distinguish what is true and just in the realm of love. Help us, heavenly guide, to foster relationships that are pure, sincere, and directed toward the glorification of God's eternal design for companionship and affection.

We pray that through your guidance, we can discern our path in love with clarity and courage. Grant us the gift of understanding, to recognize the signs that the Lord places before us, and grant us the strength to follow them. May the love we seek and nurture always be steadfast in its purpose, grounded in the virtues of patience, kindness, and selfless devotion.

Just as you have guided Tobias in his journey, accompany us, too, in our search for true companionship. Assist us in cultivating a love that is not superficial, but one that abides in the profound truths of the heart, reflective of Christ's own love for His Church. Teach us to love not only with emotion but also with the will to act justly and serve selflessly.

Watch over our decisions and the formation of our relationships, St. Raphael. Protect us from the entanglements of infatuation that lack depth and the potential to endure through life's trials. Bring to our awareness the qualities that will help us recognize God's plan for us in a life partner. Let our love for others be a testament to our love for Christ, filled with benevolence and free from every form of deceit or vanity.

In the solitude of prayer and the quiet stirrings of our hearts, we seek your intercession, St. Raphael. Steady our minds to focus on the virtues that are pleasing to God, and lead us towards a love that is reflective of divine wisdom and benevolence. With your guidance, may we find and nurture a holy bond with our future spouse, one that will be a source of joy, growth, and mutual sanctification.

Hence, we entrust to you, O Holy Archangel Raphael, our desires, our yearnings, and our quests for a love that is rooted in truth and grace. We place our confidence in your esteemed patronage as we strive to follow God's will in our relationships, assured of your support and the Lord's unending love. Amen.

Prayer for a Heart Like Ruth's - Emulating Ruth's Loyalty

Heavenly Father, in Your divine wisdom, You inspire us with stories of transformative faith and enduring love. Today, I lift my heart to You, seeking the virtues manifested in Ruth, whose loyalty and commitment have stood as an enduring example through the ages.

Grant me, O Lord, a heart like Ruth's, steadfast in devotion and rich in kindness. May I emulate her courage as she stepped into a foreign land, her life woven into the tapestry of Your greater plan. Help me to embrace the vulnerability required to love without boundaries, and to serve with the same zeal that Ruth showed to Naomi.

Saint Raphael, faithful guide, I turn to you in prayer. You are a patron to those who seek companionship and love grounded in divine grace. I ask for your intercession that I may find the fortitude to remain loyal to those I hold dear and to forge bonds of deep fidelity.

In my own search for love and connection, I pray for discernment, that I may recognize where my heart can be given fully and freely. Let your guidance lead me to a love that reflects the love Ruth had—a love that respects, honors, and uplifts. May the relationships I form be centered in mutual support and dedicated service, that together we may journey toward God's loving embrace.

May my actions embody the gentle strength and righteous character that Ruth displayed, that in all my relationships I might also be called worthy. Teach me to listen for the whispers of Your Spirit, aligning my path with Your precepts, and nurturing in me the unwavering commitment to serve.

As Ruth found refuge under the wings of the Almighty, so too do I seek Your shelter, O Lord. Bless me with a persevering spirit, and may Your divine providence guide me to the one with whom I can build a life that glorifies You.

With hope in Your unfailing love and in the compassionate care of Saint Raphael, I entrust my journey to You, O God. May my life honor the legacy of Ruth, a woman who loved deeply, acted boldly, and trusted in Your eternal faithfulness.

Through our Lord Jesus Christ, Your Son, who lives and reigns with You in the unity of the Holy Spirit, God, forever and ever. Amen.

Prayer for a Love as Strong as Jacob's - Inspired by Jacob's Love

In the quiet sanctum of my heart, where faith abides and hope blossoms, I kneel before you, Almighty God, with a request as ancient as love itself, a plea inspired by the enduring love of Jacob for his cherished Rachel. Here in your presence, I seek the intercession of St. Raphael, the guide and protector of sacred unions, as I pray for a love as steadfast and true as that which you have ordained from time immemorial.

Lord of Heaven and Earth, who looked upon Jacob's sincerity and blessed him with the devotion of his beloved, I ask that you kindle within me such clarity of heart that I may recognize and cherish a love that is divinely inspired. Let my spirit resonate with the patience and fortitude of Jacob, who counted years as days in the fervor of his passion for Rachel.

With the same intensity as the waters that Jacob once drew to nourish the flocks, may the streams of divine grace enrich my soul and guide my steps toward a companion with whom I can fulfill your purpose. Bless me, O God, with the wisdom to discern your will, the courage to embrace the path you lay before me, and the strength to uphold love's commitments through trials and joys alike.

St. Raphael, heavenly matchmaker who leads hearts to discover God's gift of love, guide me in my journey to find the one with whom I can build a life that reflects the steadfastness of Jacob's vow. Let my eyes be open to the inner beauty and virtue that draw souls together in a bond of mutual respect, understanding, and affection.

Merciful Father, as you opened Leah's womb and remembered Rachel, open the avenues of my own life that I may receive the blessing of a partner whose soul harmonizes with mine.

Teach me to love with purity, sacrifice without counting the cost, and join with another not merely in emotion but in spirit, in service to your kingdom. Let ours be a love founded on the rock of faith, shielded by hope, and illuminated by the same divine light that guided Jacob through his trials and triumphs.

And should I, like Jacob, find myself wrestling in the lonely hours of uncertainty or sorrow, grant me the perseverance to hold fast to your promises until the breaking of the day. With trust in your providence, may I encounter the one for whom you have destined my heart, certain that, like Jacob and Rachel, what is joined by your hand will endure the sands of time.

God of enduring commitments and everlasting covenants, as Raphael once brought healing and joy, send now your healing love into my life. Prepare me to be a true and faithful partner, ready to uplift, support, and journey alongside the one you have selected to be my mate.

I offer this prayer with a hope as boundless as the starry skies under which Jacob dreamt of your promise. With confidence in your timing, your plan, and your perfect will, I place this yearning of my soul into your loving hands, trusting that you will guide my way to a love as abiding and sacred as Jacob's for Rachel.

Through Christ our Lord, Amen.

Prayer for Healing from Past Hurts - Inspired by Psalm 147:3

O Healing God, who mends the brokenhearted and binds up their wounds, hear our plea through the intercession of St. Raphael,

your angel of healing and guide in matters of love and companionship.

In your Scripture, we are reminded of your tender care and compassion for us.

With trustful hearts, we call upon St. Raphael to carry our prayers to your divine throne.

May his presence be a balm to the scars that past hurts have etched upon our souls.

Where there has been pain, let there be peace; where there has been rejection, let there be acceptance.

Christ be with me, Christ within me, Christ behind me, charting a path of new beginnings.

Christ before me, guiding my steps towards love that reflects Your own.

Christ beside me, steadying me when memories of hurt emerge unbidden.

Christ to comfort and restore me, Christ beneath me, lifting me from despair,

Christ above me, reminding me of the eternal love that overshadows every earthly trial.

Christ in quiet, Christ in danger, in the hearts of all that love me.

In the spirit of humility, we surrender our pain, asking for the grace to forgive as we have been forgiven.

May St. Raphael guide us toward your healing light and prepare us for the love you have destined us to share.

Through the intercession of St. Raphael, may we perceive your love in the kindness of friends, the smile of a stranger, and the gentleness of a heart destined to beat in unison with our own.

We praise you, God of Love, for your unending patience and the unwearied love that you pour upon us.

Bless us with strength and courage as we journey forward, trusting in your wisdom and timing.

In the unity of the Spirit, we praise you, Father, Son, and Holy Spirit, for love is your greatest commandment and our ultimate call.

In every breath we take, may we draw closer to the love that heals, uplifts, and fulfills.

We pray this in the name of Jesus Christ, our Lord and Savior.

Amen.

Prayer for Purity of Heart - Reflecting on Matthew 5:8

O St. Raphael, angelic guide of human hearts,

In the quiet gaze of morning's first light, I call upon your gentle intercession.

Bless me with a heart pure as the mountain stream, untouched by the shadows of earthly desires,

That I may see the face of God in all creation, as promised in the beatitudes.

Whisper to the winds a prayer for my spirit, so that it may rise like incense,

Unblemished, steadfast in virtue, reflecting the brilliance of a soul touched by grace.

As the dew clings to the petal, may my heart cling to what is good and true,

Seeking solace in the arms of the Almighty, in the sanctuary of a will surrendered.

Lead me, O faithful companion of the pilgrim, through the valleys of temptation and doubt,

Where the echoes of purity resonate, where love's light illuminates the path of righteousness.

Wrap me in the mantle of chastity, like the lilies that dress the fields in splendor,

Free from the snares of the transient, anchored in the eternal embrace of the Divine.

In your companionship, St. Raphael, may I find the courage to conquer every impure thought,

To walk in humble service, reflecting the purity of heart that beholds God's presence.

Be my guide, as I journey towards the heart that is made for me, fashioned by Heaven's hand,

That together we may mirror the love that is unblemished, the love that transcends time.

Through your intercession, let my heart become a vessel of untarnished love,

Echoing the whisper of Divine affection, the silent roar of waters deep and clear.

To love and be loved in return, with a radiance that rivals the starlit heavens—

This is my prayer, O St. Raphael, as I seek the one whom my soul loves.

Amen.

Prayer for Selfless Love - Based on 1 Corinthians 13:4-7

O Glorious St. Raphael, faithful servant of God and friend to humanity, patron of those seeking a life-companion, I implore your intercession as I yearn for the embrace of selfless love, the kind that pours forth from the heart and reflects the boundless mercy of the Divine.

Heavenly guide, you witness the wanderings of our hearts, as did the father of the prodigal son. In your wisdom, you understand the trials of the human spirit, its quest for meaning, and the genuine connection it seeks in another. So I pray, dear St. Raphael, assist me in growing in the virtues of patience and kindness, to foster within me a love that is earnest and pure.

Just as the younger son squandered his inheritance, I recognize the times I have misused the gifts of affection and trust. In moments of weakness, I have sought fulfillment outside the sacred bonds of genuine relationship, mistaking transient pleasures for the depth of true love. Through your guidance, may I return to the path of righteousness, embracing the responsibilities and joys that come from a consecrated and steadfast partnership.

St. Raphael, you know well the pangs of envy and pride that can embitter the soul; lend me your strength to reject these snares. May I rejoice in the happiness of others, take no satisfaction in wrongdoing, and always seek the uplifting truth that leads to harmony. Encourage me, I pray, to bear no grudge, to be humble in manner and pure in intention as I walk in hope towards the covenant of love.

Let the story of the forgiving father renew my trust in forgiveness, both given and received. Teach me to forgive as freely as the father embraced his lost son, knowing that forgiveness is the very essence of love. May this understanding guide me as I forge a bond with another, shaping a relationship founded not on self-gain but on the mutual respect that fosters growth and unity.

May my journey toward finding my soulmate be one of transformation, learning to love with a heart that is not easily angered nor quick to take offense. I ask for the grace to always protect, to place unwavering trust in Divine will, to nourish hope in every circumstance, and to persevere through trials, just as the enduring father watched and waited for his son's return.

Dear St. Raphael, align my heart with the love that resonates through 1 Corinthians 13:4-7, so that I may encounter a companion with whom I can share a love that mirrors these divine attributes. I trust that with your intercession and God's ever-present assistance, our union will be a testament to the sanctity and fullness of love that is patient, kind, righteous, and enduring.

I entrust this prayer to you, St. Raphael, confident in your advocacy and in the hope that through your guidance, I may one day join hands with my soulmate in a lifetime of selfless love. Amen.

Prayer for Wisdom in Relationships - Inspired by James 1:5

O Divine Architect of Relationships, hear my earnest plea,

In your boundless mercy, intercede for me, Saint Raphael.

From the wellspring of wisdom, James reminds us to seek,

Grant me the insight required, strength when I am weak.

In my quest for companionship, guide me with celestial light,

Navigate my heart to discern, between wrong and the right.

Bestow upon me the grace, to understand and to know,

The path that leads to unity, where genuine love can grow.

Blessed healer and guardian, in love's intricate dance,

Instruct my spirit gently, fortify my advance.

Amid the ebb and flow of human ties and rapport,

Let wisdom be my anchor, now and forevermore.

In tender moments when shadows obscure the way,

Illuminate my journey, turn the night into day.

Foster within me patience, virtue that is rare,

Infuse my soul with prudence, for relationships I care.

Saint Raphael, angelic guide in the pursuit of love's quest,

Through your intercession, may my bonds be among the blessed.

May my actions reflect the love that is true and divine,

And in each encounter, let heaven's wisdom shine.

Let every word spoken, every silence held dear,

Be a testament to wisdom, dispelling all fear.

May the love I give and take, be sincere and just,

Rooted in mutual respect, and in unwavering trust.

Through your guidance, Saint Raphael, may I find the one,

Whose presence in my life, reflects the radiant sun.

Together may we journey, toward the everlasting light,

Harmonized in wisdom, in the Almighty's sight.

With a humble heart, this prayer I now convey,

Saint Raphael, bring wisdom to my relationships, I pray.

In companionship and love, may I embody peace,

And in seeking my soulmate, may my wisdom increase. Amen.

Prayer for a Faithful Partner - Reflecting on Proverbs 31

O Glorious St. Raphael, angelic healer and guide, entrusted by God to lead the faithful to righteousness and companionship, hear our humble prayer. In the spirit of Proverbs 31, we seek your heavenly intercession for the blessing of a faithful partner in life.

In the wisdom shared by King Lemuel, taught by a loving mother, we are reminded of the virtues that form the foundation of a steadfast love and the essence of a noble character. May we aspire to these graces in ourselves and desire them in the one whom God has destined for us.

We beseech thee, gentle St. Raphael, to be our advocate, as we journey in search of a heart that reflects the trustworthiness, diligence, and generosity embodied in a worthy woman—a heart honorable and true, a spirit generous and kind.

Let us pray for discernment, that we might recognize the companion who, like the woman of valor, engages in life with strength, dignity, and wisdom. May our future union be one of mutual respect, where both are empowered to serve and uplift, extending hands to the poor and open arms to the needy, enriching the world and reflecting the divine love that called us into being.

Grant us patience as we wait for this sacred connection, and let us cultivate virtues within ourselves that will one day bless a shared household—virtues that neither charm nor beauty can surpass, but a reverent fear of the Lord that ensures praise and honor.

Through your intercession, may we find the path to a love that is selfless, a partnership that prospers in faithfulness, and a shared life that glorifies the designs of the Most High. May our future union stand testament not to temporal allure, but to the lasting treasure of a God-centered bond.

With hopeful hearts, we place this petition in your hands, St. Raphael. May your guidance lead us to a love that echoes the divine, and may our lives, joined in holy companionship, shine with the true beauty of a faith-filled love that inspires and endures.

Amen.

Prayer for God-Centered Love - Based on Ecclesiastes 4:12

Let me seek You first in all things, O Lord, and let my love be but a reflection of Your divine care.

Let me find in Your providence the path to a God-centered affection, where two souls might strive together, not alone, and truly manifest the strength of a threefold cord that cannot quickly be broken, as Your wisdom proclaims in Ecclesiastes.

Let me not chase the passing whispers of selfish love, but rather yearn for a bond that echoes Your sacrificial heart.

Let me acknowledge my weaknesses, so in my seeking, I might be drawn to one who complements, not merely reflects, so together we grow towards You.

Let me cherish humility, so pride does not overshadow the call to serve within love's gentle fold.

Let me be patient, trusting Your timing over my own, and in this waiting, let my heart be prepared like fertile ground for the seed of true companionship You design.

Let me be guided by the light of St. Raphael, whose wisdom unveils the holy union destined by Your will.

Let me honor the sanctity of a union that seeks first Your kingdom, knowing that all else shall be added unto us.

Let me embrace a love that bears all things, believes all things, hopes all things, endures all things, love that mirrors Your unfailing nature.

Let me, through intercessory prayer, find solace in St. Raphael's guidance, who aids those in search of a sacred partnership.

Let me love not just in word or speech, but in truth and action, so this God-centered love may be a testament, not of my desires, but of Your glory.

Let me preserve this love not as a fragile glass, easily shattered, but as a resilient bond, fortified by grace and destined by Your sovereign hand.

And finally, let me keep love's flame burning brightly, a beacon of Your presence in a world that so often forgets Your commandments of love.

May St. Raphael intercede on my behalf, that I may one day stand beside my soulmate, hands joined, hearts united, in perfect harmony with Your divine plan. Amen.

Prayer for Overcoming Obstacles in Love - Inspired by Romans 8:28

O loving St. Raphael, angelic healer and guide, with a heart full of trust in the divine promise that all things work together for good for those who love God, we reach out to you in prayer. We seek your intercession, as we navigate the obstacles that stand before us in our pursuit of love, that we may be imbued with the same faith and endurance that graced Joseph amidst his trials.

Just as Joseph, when betrayed by his brothers and enveloped by the chains of injustice, saw beyond his sufferings to the unfolding of God's gracious plan, we too ask for the grace to persevere through the challenges that love entails. May we hold fast to hope, understanding that our present struggles in love can become the foundation upon which a greater love is built, as intended by the One who calls us according to His purpose.

We ask you, St. Raphael, to carry our prayers to the throne of mercy, that we may find strength to forgive those who may have caused our hearts to grieve, much like Joseph forgave his brothers, recognizing the hand of God at work even in our deepest pain. In this forgiveness, may our hearts be open to the healing and unity that true love seeks to foster.

Guide us, dear St. Raphael, on the path to a love that is patient, kind, and free from the snares of envy and pride. Help us to foster relationships grounded in the trust in God's providence, remembering always that our current struggles can be stepping stones toward greater intimacy and joy.

Through your intercession, may we embrace the wisdom to discern the difference between fleeting discomforts and the genuine obstacles that require our courageous action or patient endurance. Teach us the ways of love that is selfless and enduring, mirroring the divine love that perseveres through all trials.

We place our trust in your guidance, St. Raphael, as we seek to overcome the hurdles before us, that in all our loving endeavors, we may ultimately realize the profound truth that lies within our trials, finding peace and solace in the knowledge that, with God, all things lead to good for those who love Him.

Amen.

Prayer for Unity in Future Relationship - Reflecting on Ephesians 4:2-3

O Holy St. Raphael, patron of those seeking a mate,

I come before you, seeking your guidance and intercession

In the hopeful anticipation of a future relationship founded on unity and love.

May your prayers join mine as I aspire for a bond reflective of Ephesians 4:2-3,

To live "with all humility and gentleness, with patience, bearing with one another in love,"

And to strive for the unity of the Spirit in the peace that binds us.

I pray for the wisdom to live out these virtues in my future relationship,

To foster a patient heart, a humble spirit, and an enduring love;

Qualities that kept Abraham and Sarah together despite their trials.

Like them, who navigated the uncertainty of their promise with faith,

I desire to build a future partnership grounded in mutual respect and divine trust.

May the same commitment to Your divine will that guided them,

Reign in my future relationship, through every challenge it may face.

Grant me, St. Raphael, the grace to recognize and nurture,

A bond that carries the kind of love that reflects God's own,

One that grows stronger through every joy and obstacle shared.

May our union be a testament to God's loving providence,

A unity that mirrors the promised fulfillment bestowed upon Abraham and Sarah,

Filled with the perseverance that comes from a shared belief in God's promises.

St. Raphael, guide our paths towards each other,

And protect our future union with your prayers,

That we may rejoice in a relationship that glorifies God

Through a love that embodies humility, patience, and peace.

Amen.

Prayer for Finding Joy in Love - Based on Psalm 37:4

O Glorious St. Raphael, faithful servant of the Most High and heavenly guide of those seeking companionship, hear our earnest plea. In the spirit of the Psalmist, who taught us to delight in the Lord, we seek your intercession that we, too, might find joy in the love ordained for us by our Creator.

Just as you led Tobias to Sarah, binding them with the unbreakable bond of holy matrimony, guide us to recognize the divine love crafted for our lives. May our hearts, full of faith, be attuned to the gentle whispers of God's Spirit, steering us toward a love that echoes the sacred unity of Isaac and Rebekah.

Through your intercession, St. Raphael, may we, like Abraham's servant, approach the task of finding a lifetime partner with humility and trust. Grant us the wisdom to seek not only outward beauty but inner grace, hospitality, and kindness, which stem from a heart in tune with God's own.

As we journey toward the flourishing of love, let patience steady our anxious minds and kindle within us the burning light of hope. Cast away the shadows of doubt and the fear of loneliness, instilling in us an unwavering trust in the Father's timing and providence.

St. Raphael, as you once guided with the light of heaven, illuminate now our path, that we may encounter the soul appointed to journey with us toward eternity. And in the finding, may our union become a testament to the joy that blooms when two hearts align beneath God's gaze.

We ask you to carry our prayers to the throne of the Almighty, that in aligning our desires with God's divine will, we may, as the Psalmist declares, receive the desires of our heart—desires purified, uplifted, and made holy through our delight in the Lord.

O blessed St. Raphael, imbue our hearts with the courage to pursue a love that mirrors the selfless love of Christ. Let this pursuit not be for fulfillment alone but for a shared call to sanctity and service, where joy is found not in possession but in mutual giving and in the unwavering commitment to one another's salvation.

With devout hearts, we thank you, St. Raphael, for your heavenly aid. Continue to be our advocate and friend, and may the joy we seek in love be a reflection of the eternal love that God has for each of His children. Through your intercession, may our lives be blessed with the grace to love fully, deeply, and with the boundlessness with which we are loved by our Father in Heaven.

Amen.

Prayer for Humility in Love - Inspired by Philippians 2:3

O Holy St. Raphael, guide of those seeking true companionship and patron of loving relationships, I come before you in search of your gentle intercession. I am inspired by the wise words in Philippians 2:3, which teaches us to act not out of selfish ambition or vain conceit, but instead to carry a spirit of humility, valuing others more than ourselves. In this journey towards love, I seek the grace to embody these sacred teachings.

Please St. Raphael, I humbly ask you to aid my heart in recognizing the sacred echo of divine love that flourished when Jesus, our teacher, lovingly washed the feet of His disciples. On that holy evening during the Last Supper, He took upon Himself the humblest of services to show the depth and purity of His love. May this act of Jesus instill in me the same humility and willingness to serve within my own relationships, especially in my quest for a soulmate.

As I seek a partner with whom to share my life, encourage me to prioritize their needs, to listen deeply, and to walk with them in selflessness and generosity. Let my affection be marked not by what I can gain, but by what I can give. Allow me the vision to see beyond my desires, focusing instead on creating a foundation of mutual support and respect.

St. Raphael, in your loving wisdom, guide my actions and my words, so that my love may reflect the humility of Christ. Teach me the virtue of patience, the strength to be vulnerable, and the courage to uplift my future partner in their endeavors, celebrating their achievements as if they were my own. Assist me in understanding that true humility is not thinking less of myself, but thinking of myself less.

I ask you, St. Raphael, to pray for me as I strive to cultivate a love as pure and selfless as the Savior's. Protect my journey towards a fulfilling relationship with the hand of God guiding us towards unity and understanding. Help me to be a reflection of Christ's love, offering tenderness and compassion to all whom I encounter, especially the one who you, in your holy guidance, will lead into my life as a loving companion.

Through your intercession, St. Raphael, may the seeds of humility in love be deeply planted within my spirit, blooming into a bond that glorifies God and embodies the essence of Christian love. May my heart always mirror the profound humility of Christ, and through this prayer, may the path to my future soulmate be blessed with the radiance of divine grace and guided by the wisdom of God's will.

Amen.

Prayer for Strength in Singlehood - Reflecting on Isaiah 40:31

O St. Raphael, beloved archangel and patron of happy encounters,

Hear this prayer for strength in the quiet meadows of singlehood.

As the scripture sings in Isaiah, those who hope in the Lord will renew their strength,

So empower me to soar on wings like eagles, to run and not grow weary.

Amidst the solace of my solitude, guide my heart with celestial tenderness,

For in the embrace of divine grace, my spirit finds the courage to stand alone.

Yet, in the tranquil silence of this journey, I seek the whispers of divine companionship,

With you, St. Raphael, as my faithful advocate in the courts of Heaven.

I pray for resilience that flows like a river through the soul,

As each step taken is a verse in the anthem of my unwritten destiny.

Grant me sight, O healer of the blind, to see the beauty woven in the tapestries of time,

Where love is not a fleeting shadow, but a light that beckons with patience.

May your gentle intercession be the wind beneath my quest,

Aiding me in threading the needle of life with threads of joy and purpose.

In singlehood's silent sacrament, may I be enveloped in comfort and peace,

For in the furnace of solitude, ironclad strength and character are forged.

With celestial guidance, may my path align with one whose soul resonates in harmony,

In a symphony of shared dreams, where two stars dance in the vast expanse of possibility.

Until that ordained moment of divine union, protect my heart,

That it may remain open and unscathed by the storms of transient desire.

In your hands, I place my hope, St. Raphael, companion of the solitary heart,

That through your angelic guidance, I navigate the waters of singlehood with grace.

May I emerge with wings of wisdom, poised for the blessing of a love divine,

For in God's time, all things converge in the splendor of His perfect will.

Amen.

Prayer for Guided Steps Towards Love - Based on Psalm 37:23

In the quiet journey of the heart, where love seeks its kindred spirit,

And within the tumult of life, where paths cross and tangle,

I seek your intercession, St. Raphael, guide of the faithful and friend of the lonely.

When uncertainty clouds my vision and doubt creeps into my resolve,

Lead me, through your gentle advocacy, to the certainty of God's perfect plan.

As I wander in the wilderness of singleness, guide my steps towards an encounter with true love.

Where fear speaks louder than hope, and isolation wraps its grip around me,

Whisper into my life the words of Psalm 37:23 – that the Lord directs the steps of the godly.

May I trust in the divine rhythm, the unseen choreography that guides me to the one my soul loves.

When solitude presses heavy and my heart longs for companionship,

Implore, for me, the grace of patience, that I may wait with a spirit of joyful expectation.

Encourage me to cultivate a love that is selfless, and in the meantime, to embrace the growth solitude brings.

In moments I am tempted to mold love to my will, rather than to discover its natural form,

Remind me that true love cannot be forced or hurried, but awaits in the fullness of time.

Let my affection not be a mirror solely seeking its reflection, but a window opening to the light of another soul.

As I seek not just to be loved, but to love generously in return,

Teach me the art of self-giving, knowing that in giving we receive, in forgiving we are forgiven.

In the measure I pour out my heart, may it be filled in return, drawing ever nearer to the love God has prepared for me.

St. Raphael, companion on the journey, bearer of healing and hope,

Intercede for me, that love might be both my destination and my way.

May my steps be steady and my heart prepared for this most sacred of human bonds. Amen.

Prayer for Forgiveness in Relationships - Inspired by Colossians 3:13

O Blessed St. Raphael, patron of those seeking companionship and healing, we humbly seek your intercession as we navigate the intricate paths of our relationships. Lend us your guidance, so that we may embrace the wisdom of Colossians 3:13, to bear with one another and, if one has a complaint against another, to forgive each other just as the Lord forgave us.

In our human frailty, we acknowledge the times we have harbored resentment, allowed anger to dictate our actions, and withheld the grace of forgiveness from those who have wronged us. We recall the teaching of the Unforgiving Servant, and the boundless mercy shown by the king within that parable – a mirror to the infinite compassion of our Creator.

We ask for the strength to reflect divine mercy in our daily interactions, to forgive not merely seven times, but seventy times seven, holding no record of wrongs but striving to mirror Your inexhaustible forgiveness. May our hearts not be hardened like the unforgiving servant, but be softened by the recognition of our own need for pardon and the comfort of God's unending love and forgiveness.

Grant us the courage, dear St. Raphael, to reconcile with those we have hurt and to seek forgiveness from those we have wronged, fostering healing where there has been pain. Allow us to let go of past grievances and to approach each interaction with a spirit of understanding and a readiness to forgive, just as we seek to be forgiven.

May our relationships be sanctified by the peace that comes

from true forgiveness, nourished by God's grace, and guided by Your gentle hand. As we move forward, let us remember that forgiveness is not a singular act, but a continual process that transforms the soul and draws us ever closer to the loving heart of the Almighty.

St. Raphael, guide us on this journey towards wholeness and unity, knowing that when we forgive from the heart, we open ourselves to the possibility of a love that knows no bounds – the very love that God has for each of us. May our lives be testaments to the power of forgiveness, and may our love for one another be a reflection of God's eternal love for us. Amen.

Prayer for a Partnership of Mutual Respect - Reflecting on 1 Peter 3:7

Heavenly Father, in the tender embrace of your divine love, we find the strength and wisdom to exercise patience, kindness, and mutual respect within our partnerships. Today, we turn our hearts towards the example of St. Raphael, seeking his intercessory guidance on our journey towards creating and nurturing relationships founded on these sacred virtues.

Guided by the spirit of 1 Peter 3:7, we humbly ask that you infuse our partnerships with understanding and an unyielding reverence for one another. May we, like Joseph, approach each other with the same gentleness and protective concern, seeing beyond our own challenges to uphold the dignity of our partners.

Lord, we implore you to breathe your life-giving spirit into every interaction, so that we may honor you in our efforts to build a partnership of mutual respect. Grant us the grace to communicate with compassion, to listen deeply beyond words, and to respond with the wisdom that Joseph exhibited in his merciful discretion towards Mary.

In our moments of doubt and uncertainty, may we seek the counsel of St. Raphael, who guides souls towards thoughtful companionship. Let our actions reflect a profound respect for the divine plan you have envisioned for us, mirroring the trust that Joseph placed in your angelic messenger's revelation.

We pray for the courage to face societal pressures and personal fears with a serenity that springs from faith in your goodness. By St. Raphael's intercession, may our relationship be a testament to your desire for our joy and the sanctity of love grounded in mutual admiration.

Father, we believe in your promise of guidance and support. May we always endeavor to be true partners, offering each other the patience, understanding, and respect that you have so graciously extended to all your children. In our daily walk with one another, help us to reflect divine grace, just as Mary and Joseph modeled grace under circumstances of trial and trust.

Through St. Raphael's intercession, and in the name of Your Son, Jesus Christ, we pray for relationships characterized by such enduring mutual respect, that they reveal to the world the transformative power of your love. Amen.

Prayer for a Loving Heart - Based on 1 Samuel 16:7

O Glorious St. Raphael, celestial healer and guide of those who journey in search of companionship,

We come before you, seeking your intercession for a loving and understanding heart.

As you minister in God's presence, we pray you hear our supplications and carry them to the Almighty,

For it is in the quiet chambers of the heart that true love is discerned,

And by divine wisdom, not by sight, that souls are bonded in grace and purpose.

St. Raphael, you who bind the hearts of men and women in holy unity,

Impart to us the discernment of the Lord, who sees not as man sees,

Whose gaze pierces through outer appearances to the truth hidden within,

As proclaimed in the words of Scripture, "The Lord looks at the heart."

May we, too, look beyond the superficial and perceive with a heart fashioned by God's own hand.

Guide us, St. Raphael, in nurturing a spirit ripe with compassion and understanding,

In being patient and kind, free from envy, boastfulness, and pride.

Help us strip away the veils of judgment and fear that obstruct the light of true love,

For in embracing understanding, we mirror the infinite charity of Christ.

Grant, O faithful St. Raphael, that our hearts may be sanctuaries of love's divine essence,

Living temples where understanding and empathy flourish,

Where the goodness of souls is cherished and the will of God prevails.

In your goodness, St. Raphael, journey with us in seeking a soulmate who reflects God's love,

One with whom we may share a lifetime, discerned through divine wisdom and enlightened by mutual respect.

May our hearts unite under God's watchful eye, a testament to the spiritual bond created by His hand.

Through your intercession, kind St. Raphael, may our heartbeats echo the rhythm of God's own heart,

In love and understanding, until the end of our days,

And thereafter, in the celestial harmony of His eternal kingdom.

Amen.

Protection from Deceptive Love - Inspired by Ephesians 6:10-18

Heavenly Father, I come before You in humble trust, seeking the intercession of St. Raphael, Your faithful servant and guide in matters of the heart. Grant me, I pray, discernment that I might recognize the truth of love, shielded from deceit and shadow.

In a world where emotions can be clouded and intentions skewed, I implore You to wrap me in the mantle of Your divine wisdom. Let St. Raphael stand beside me, a beacon of Your purity, guiding my steps away from the snares of deceptive love.

Fortify my spirit with the armor of faith, as described in Ephesians, that I may withstand the temptations that lead me astray. May St. Raphael defend my heart with the sword of truth and the shield of heavenly grace. Let Your light illuminate my path, that I might love not in blindness but with the clarity of Your sight.

With every breath, I seek Your protection, for in You alone I find the safe harbor of authentic love. Empower me, through St. Raphael's intercession, to love with a love that echoes Your own—a love sincere, selfless, and sanctified.

And when uncertainty seeks to overpower me, draw me closer to Your embrace, where true love originates and eternally endures. Through St. Raphael's guidance, lead me to the one whom my soul seeks, the one You have destined for me to cherish.

In my moments of weakness, be my strength; in my confusions, be my certainty. May Your will be the compass of my journey, the promise of an undivided heart that seeks first

Your kingdom and Your righteousness.

Through the intercession of St. Raphael, let Your encompassing peace be the sentinel of my soul, and may the companionship I find honor You in its purity and joy. In faith and patience, I await Your providence, for with You, all things are woven in the fullness of time.

Amen.

Prayer for a Relationship Built on Faith - Reflecting on Hebrews 11:1

Heavenly Father, originator of love and architect of the sacred bond of marriage, I approach You with a trusting heart. Your Word, in Hebrews 11:1, assures us that faith is the confidence in what we hope for and the assurance about what we do not see. With this promise cradled in my soul, I humbly seek Your guidance for a relationship founded on unwavering faith.

Lord Jesus Christ, Your love is the wellspring of all true affection. Amidst life's complexities, I yearn for a companion with whom to share a love reflective of Your sacrificial devotion. Grant me the patience to await this gift and the wisdom to discern Your hand in its unfolding.

Holy Spirit, Comforter and Counselor, imbue me with the serenity that arises from faith in God's perfect timing. Nurture within me a fruitful spirit, that I might grow in virtue and readiness for the love ordained for me. Kindle within my heart an unshakeable trust in God's plan, free from restlessness and doubt.

Blessed Virgin Mary, model of fidelity and grace, your unwavering trust in God's will is a beacon to those navigating the voyage of the heart. Intercede for me, that I may emulate your pure and trusting heart, embracing God's will with joyful hope and serene countenance.

St. Raphael, healer and guide of lovers, as you once guided Tobias, I beseech you to steer my steps towards a companion destined for me by divine providence. Uphold me in the quest for a love that mirrors the unity and selflessness celebrated in the communion of saints.

Holy Archangels, Michael, defender of the faithful, Gabriel, messenger of good news, Raphael, patron of happy encounters, your luminous presence dispels the shadows of uncertainty. I implore your collective intercession that my path to love may be safeguarded from doubt and illuminated by faith-filled assurance.

Communion of Saints, witnesses of the transformative power of divine love, envelop me in your prayers. May your heavenly fellowship remind me that love on earth can draw its strength and inspiration from the eternal.

Lord, though I walk through seasons of solitude, let not my heart grow wary. Instead, let me be filled with hope that rests on the promise of unseen things. Even in the silent embrace of waiting, may Your peace resonate within me, echoing the wholeness found in You alone.

Divine Trinity, Father, Son, and Holy Spirit, in Your perfect communion lies the blueprint for all human connection. Instill in me the fortitude to build a relationship that is steeped in faith - one that stands unshaken amid the vicissitudes of life, and shines as a testament to Your unfailing love.

In Jesus' name, I pray, Amen.

Prayer for Gratitude in Love's Journey - Based on 1 Thessalonians 5:18

Heavenly Father, gracious and loving Lord,

In every step of love's intricate journey, we turn to You with hearts brimming with gratitude. For in the fabric of our lives, every thread is woven by Your divine providence, each moment a testament to Your perfect timing. We give thanks in all circumstances, as You taught us through Your apostle Paul, for this is Your will for us in Christ Jesus.

St. Raphael, angel of happy meetings, we ask for your intercession. Guide our hearts to understand the value of patience, as we seek the companionship destined for us. May we cherish the solitude and the introspections it offers as much as the joy of togetherness, learning to grow in self-love so that we may better love another.

Lord Jesus, You have shown us the ultimate act of love in Your sacrifice. May we emulate Your unconditional love, recognizing that even in the absence of human affection, we are forever embraced by Your divine love. Help us to remember that our worth is not dependent on another but is found in You alone.

Grant us the wisdom, dear God, to discern the difference between transient infatuation and abiding love, the courage to let go when necessary, and the hope to embrace new beginnings. May our gratitude extend beyond the joyful unions and endure through the times of loss and longing, for even in these, there is purpose and a chance for our hearts to draw nearer to You.

In moments when we question Your plan, remind us of Your faithfulness. Teach us to trust in Your impeccable timing, for

You see the entirety of our lives when we see but a fraction. May our souls rest in the assurance that in Your vast tapestry, each detail is crafted with intention and love.

O St. Raphael, journey with us as we navigate the pathways of the heart. Through your guidance, lead us to the love that reflects the light of Christ, a love born of virtue and sustained by grace. And as we traverse these varied paths, let gratitude illuminate our way, for even in waiting, there is much to be thankful for.

We pray, knowing that whether we walk alone or beside another, Your love, O God, is the source from which all true love flows. With grateful hearts, we rejoice in the journey, for in every joy and sorrow, in every high and low, Your love remains steadfast.

We close this prayer in the name of Jesus Christ, our Savior and greatest example of love, through whom all good things come, confident that Your will is ever guiding us to the love that endures, the love that is true.

Amen.

Prayer for Divine Timing in Love - Inspired by Ecclesiastes 3:1

There is a time for everything, and a season for every activity under the heavens:

We come before you, St. Raphael, seeking your intercession as we navigate the path of love, trusting in the divine timing that organizes our lives.

Guide us, that we may be patient and attentive to the signs and whispers of God's will in our journey toward finding our soulmate.

There is a time for everything, and a season for every activity under the heavens:

In moments of solitude, may we find the strength to prepare our hearts for the love that awaits us. We ask you, St. Raphael, to help us cultivate self-understanding, compassion, and virtue, essential for the love that we will share with another soul.

There is a time for everything, and a season for every activity under the heavens:

As we walk through different seasons of relationship, from friendship to profound connection, may your guidance, St. Raphael, lead us to recognize the bonds that are meant to flourish. Help us to discern which relationships are nurturing and will bear the fruits of a lasting commitment.

There is a time for everything, and a season for every activity under the heavens:

In times of anticipation, keep us from haste and remind us of the gentle pace of grace. May your support, St. Raphael, foster patience and trust in us, as we embrace the natural unfolding of love in God's perfect timing.

There is a time for everything, and a season for every activity under the heavens:

When we are weary from waiting or disheartened by past disappointments, inspire us with renewed hope. Through your intercession, St. Raphael, may we be uplifted by the promise that God's plans for us are woven with wisdom and care.

There is a time for everything, and a season for every activity under the heavens:

Bless our future unions with the light of understanding and the warmth of mutual respect. May the love we find be grounded in faith and grow to reflect the unending love that God has for each of us.

There is a time for everything, and a season for every activity under the heavens:

St. Raphael, patron of loving companionship and healing, intercede for us that when the time is right, our hearts will be ready to welcome the love that is destined for us. In God's harmony, may we find our soulmate and embark upon a journey that honors the sacred essence of companionship.

Amen.

Embracing God's Will in Marriage - Reflecting on Matthew 6:10

O Loving and Tender God, who art in heaven, we humbly stand before You and embrace Your holy will for the sacrament of marriage, which You have ordained as a sacred union between two souls.

With humbled hearts, we reflect on the joyous wedding at Cana, where Your Son, Jesus, was present and performed His first public miracle, turning water into wine. It is here that we see the care You have for all aspects of our lives, including those moments of celebration in marital love.

Blessed St. Raphael, angel of happy meetings, we invite your gentle intercession. With maternal instincts, Mary sought Jesus's help at Cana, trustingly interceding for the needs of the couple. In similar faith, we ask you, St. Raphael, to guide us in recognizing and fulfilling God's will within our own marriages and relationships.

May we, like the servants at Cana, listen attentively to Your voice, O Lord, and do whatever You instruct, confident that You will provide for our needs. Let Your grace fill our lives with the richness of new wine—joy, peace, and love—fostering a bond that mirrors the communion of the Holy Trinity.

Instill in us, dear Lord, the virtues of patience, understanding, and unwavering commitment to one another. Just as Mary believed in the power of Your Son's divine will, let us trust in Your perfect design for our marriage, always open to the work You wish to do through us and in us.

May every married couple strive to invite Jesus into their lives, ensuring His presence is the cornerstone of their relationship.

Let our love for one another be a sign to the world of Your love for Your Church, a testament to the joy and the celebration that is found in a life shared in Christ.

Through the example of the Holy Family, teach us to love selflessly, to serve joyously, and to cherish each moment we are given together. And may the powerful intercession of St. Raphael, the patron of those seeking a marriage partner, lead us closer to the Divine Love that You have laid out for us from the beginning of time.

Grant, we pray, that as we grow in love for each other, we may also grow in love for You, dear Lord, embracing with grace every challenge and joy that comes our way. In our journey together, let Your will be done on earth, as it is in heaven, for in Your divine will is our peace and ultimate joy.

Amen.

Thank you Lord...

_____
_____
_____
_____
_____
_____
_____
_____
_____
_____

St. Raphael, please intercede for me...

_____
_____
_____
_____
_____
_____
_____
_____
_____
_____

My personal prayer...

_____
_____
_____
_____
_____
_____
_____
_____
_____
_____

My prayer for my loved ones...

_____
_____
_____
_____
_____
_____
_____
_____
_____
_____

My current challenges...

_____
_____
_____
_____
_____
_____
_____
_____
_____
_____

Lord, offer me guidance...

_____
_____
_____
_____
_____
_____
_____
_____
_____
_____

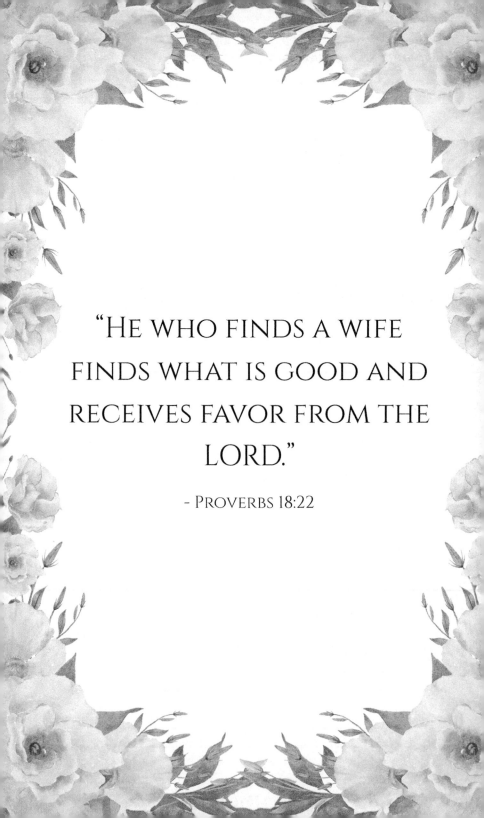

"HE WHO FINDS A WIFE
FINDS WHAT IS GOOD AND
RECEIVES FAVOR FROM THE
LORD."

- PROVERBS 18:22

Novena

Introduction

As we open our hearts to the sacred tradition of novena, we embark upon a nine-day spiritual journey, seeking the intercession of St. Raphael the Archangel in our profound quest for companionship. This novena is a resolute call to the heavens, uniting our fervent prayers with the compassionate advocacy of our celestial guide.

For nine days, we will reflect upon the virtues and deeds of St. Raphael, drawing inspiration from his divine role in the Book of Tobit. Each day of our novena will bring us closer to understanding his celestial guidance and the spiritual dimensions of true love. Through this prayerful endeavor, we are not simply reciting words; we are weaving a tapestry of faith that seeks the blessing of a sacred and lasting bond.

St. Raphael, whose name means "God Heals," is not only a healer of the body but also a curative balm for the soul, especially in matters of the heart. As Tobit and Sarah were brought to a holy union through his intercession, we too seek his heavenly assistance in finding our life's partner, the one whom God has destined for us.

With each day's dedicated prayer, we grow in devotion and trust, forging a spiritual connection that transcends the boundaries of earth. As we utter these prayers, let us be mindful of the divine power available to us in our supplication. Let our voices be heard in unison, and our intentions be as clear as the light of God's own truth as we seek St. Raphael's guidance in finding our soulmate.

Thank you Lord for...

_____
_____
_____
_____
_____
_____
_____
_____
_____
_____
_____
_____
_____

My personal novena intentions...

_____
_____
_____
_____
_____
_____
_____
_____
_____
_____
_____
_____
_____
_____
_____
_____
_____
_____

My intentions for humanity...

_____
_____
_____
_____
_____
_____
_____
_____
_____
_____
_____
_____
_____

My novena intentions for my loved ones...

_____
_____
_____
_____
_____
_____
_____
_____
_____
_____
_____
_____
_____
_____
_____

First Day

Let us begin our novena with hearts open to the transformative power of God's divine plan, seeking the intercession of St. Raphael, our guide and protector on our journey towards love.

In the Name of the Father, and of the Son, and of the Holy Spirit. Amen.

Dear Heavenly Father, creator of all that is good and loving, we come before you today with humble hearts, filled with desire to find the soulmate you have destined for us. We praise you for your infinite wisdom and your matchless power to bring souls together in love.

We invoke the holy intercession of St. Raphael, your faithful Archangel, who holds the esteemed title of "God heals" and "Medicine of God." We honor his roles as healer of the Earth and patron of those seeking a life partner. St. Raphael, you who arranged the beautiful marriage of Tobias and Sarah, guide us, as you did with them, through the trials and uncertainties that cloud our vision.

Almighty God, you know the depths of our hearts and the longing we carry for companionship and love. We ask that, through the intercession of St. Raphael, you grace us with the clarity to perceive your divine will in our lives. May the eyes of our hearts be enlightened, that we may understand the hopes to which you have called us, and recognize the presence of our future spouse whom you have prepared for us.

Glorious St. Raphael, lead us as you led Tobias, accompany us on our journey and direct our steps towards God's grace. Clear the path of any obstacle that may prevent us from meeting our soulmate and heal any wound that hinders us from being able to give and receive love fully.

Prayer to St. Raphael:

Glorious St. Raphael, Archangel of healing and herald of divine love, we earnestly implore your powerful intercession. With your guidance, may we navigate the complexities of relationships with courage and purity of heart. Teach us to love ourselves as vessels of God's will, that we may be ready to welcome the soulHe has chosen for us. Assist us in casting aside doubts and grant us the wisdom to recognize the sanctity of the union that awaits us.

May our hearts be open to the lessons we must learn, and our spirits be patient in the unfoldment of God's timing. We trust in your caring assistance and your prayers before the Throne of God.

Day by Day Prayer:

Dearest St. Raphael, I beseech you to offer my prayers to God on this first day of our novena, as I request clarity and wisdom in my search for love. I pray that my future spouse and I may be drawn together as part of His divine plan, forming a bond that reflects the love and compassion emblematic of a Christ-centered relationship.

We conclude our prayers with hope, invoking your angelic strength and guidance, St. Raphael. Through your intercession, may we achieve the blessedness of finding our soulmate, and through this divine partnership, may we advance closer to God's love.

Amen.

Second Day

Let us begin in stillness, recalling the serene patience of St. Raphael as he walked alongside Tobiah, guiding him through his quest with enduring faithfulness. On this day, we embrace the tranquility and strength found in the virtue of patience and the unwavering trust that we, too, are accompanied by a heavenly guide on our path to love.

In the Name of the Father, and of the Son, and of the Holy Spirit. Amen.

Merciful and Patient Lord,

Who in Your infinite wisdom, understand all the seasons of our lives,

We come before You seeking the grace to cultivate patience,

As we journey towards the heart destined to beat in unison with our own.

St. Raphael, faithful companion of Tobiah,

You traversed great distances, your presence an unfaltering beacon of support.

Impart upon us your serene composure as we encounter the ebbs and flows of the heart,

Teaching us to wait with grace for the tapestry of destiny to be woven by the Divine Hand.

In moments of eagerness, when the soul grows restless for companionship,

Remind us that true love is worth every second of divine orchestration,

That each solitary step taken is a step closer to the ordained meeting decreed from Heaven.

Glorious Archangel,

Instill within us a trust that is stout-hearted and devoid of doubt,

Much like Tobiah, who ventured forth, unaware of the blessings that laid ahead,

Yet held steadfast to faith under the watchful guidance of your radiant wing.

As we surrender to the profound mysteries of time and divine will,

Allow our trust in God's plan to deepen,

Knowing that each encounter, each farewell, is a note within a celestial symphony,

Leading to the moment when two souls recognize each other as lifelong melodies.

Lend us your vision to see the light of God's love, leading us faithfully towards our future union.

With every breath, may our prayers entwine with your own,

A gentle yet insistent call for celestial assistance,

For eyes to recognize God's hand in every moment and encounter,

Till at last, in the fullness of time, we stand before our soulmate,

A journey's end blessed by St. Raphael's unwavering guidance.

Through your intercession, may we find solace in the knowledge that God's timing is perfect,

And may our hearts remain open and expectant of the joyous union to come.

We pray in earnest, St. Raphael. Amen.

Third Day

As we continue our spiritual journey together, let us turn with devotion to Day 3 of our novena dedicated to St. Raphael, the Archangel of healing and patron of those seeking their soulmate. On this day, we implore his intercession to mend the fractures within our hearts, to soothe the echoes of past hurts and disappointments, and to restore us to wholeness. Let us enter this time of prayer, seeking his divine assistance in clearing the path to the love that awaits us, in God's perfect timing.

Begin with the Sign of the Cross.

In the name of the Father, and of the Son, and of the Holy Spirit. Amen.

Dear St. Raphael, companion of the journey, healer of the afflicted, you who have the power to guide and to mend, hear our prayers. We come before you with hearts that have known sorrow, with memories that at times feel like thorns within our flesh. We trust in your gentle care, O healing balm of God, to touch our tender wounds and promote within us a process of spiritual restoration.

(Reflect quietly on your past emotional hurts.)

Loving St. Raphael, you who stood by Tobias as he journeyed to find his spouse, stand by us. Guide us through the valleys of our vulnerabilities, the places where we have been broken, that we might find strength in our weaknesses and grace in our growth.

(Pray for the healing of a specific emotional hurt you have experienced.)

Precious healer, we ask that through your intercession, our Lord Jesus Christ might grant us the grace of inner healing, and that the Holy Spirit might comfort us in our struggles, enkindling within us a renewed sense of hope and joy. May our healed hearts become fertile ground for love, where trust can blossom and the integrity of a God-centered relationship can take root.

Most compassionate St. Raphael, teach us to release the pain of the past, to forgive those who have wounded us, and to forgive ourselves for our own part in these sorrows. Let us move forward, not as captives of our history, but as pilgrims intent on living in the light of God's love.

(Share a silent moment of forgiveness and letting go.)

As we journey towards the love that God has in store for us, may our hearts be open and responsive, free from the chains of bygone affections, and receptive to the gift of a soulmate who reflects the love of Christ. May our souls be attuned to the providence of God, who heals us, loves us, and prepares us for an encounter with our future spouse.

Conclude with a prayer to Our Father, Hail Mary, and Glory Be.

Our Father, Who art in Havel; Hallowed be Thy Name. Thy Kingdom come. Thy will be done, on earth as it is in Heaven. Give us this day our daily bread, and forgive us our trespasses, as we forgive those who trespass against us; and lead us not into temptation, but deliver us from evil. Amen.

Hail Mary, full of grace, the Lord is with thee; blessed art thou amongst women, and blessed is the fruit of thy womb, Jesus. Holy Mary, Mother of God, pray for us sinners, now and at the hour of our death. Amen.

Glory be to the Father, and to the Son, and to the Holy Spirit, as it was in the beginning, is now, and ever shall be, world without end. Amen.

Fourth Day

Beloved faithful, on this fourth day of our novena we gather together in spiritual communion to honor and seek the guidance of St. Raphael, the archangel who is the custodian of divine providence in the realm of sacred unions. It was St. Raphael who accompanied Tobiah on his journey, ensuring his safety and providing wise counsel. Today, we pray that we may also experience such heavenly guidance in our daily actions and the significant decisions that shape our lives on the path to finding our soulmate.

In the name of the Father, and of the Son, and of the Holy Spirit. Amen.

Let us start this day with a reflection on the holy scripture:

"Then Tobias answered the angel, 'I beg you, brother Azarias, tell me what remedies these things have that you are speaking about.' The angel replied, 'Do you not remember your father's orders? He commanded you to take a wife for yourself from your father's family. Now listen to me, brother; do not worry about this demon.'"

(Tobit 6:7-8)

As Tobiah trusted St. Raphael and followed his guidance, we, too, look to St. Raphael to steer our steps. May his celestial intercession illuminate our understanding and fortify our resolve to adhere to the virtuous path that leads to true companionship.

Let us now pray:

Glorious St. Raphael, entrusted by God with the task of assisting us in finding our way to genuine love and companionship, we ask for your guidance. Just as you directed Tobiah to his future spouse with wisdom and care, lead us toward a relationship that is nurturing, spiritually fulfilling, and in accordance with divine plan.

Dear archangel, we humbly request your heavenly assistance in every decision we make—a gentle but firm push towards the divine will, enabling us to discern wisely the choices before us. We wish for our future union to reflect God's love and to be a testament to the sanctity of marriage, as intended from the beginning of creation.

Almighty and eternal God, who through Your eternal Word has taught us that our actions must be guided by love and directed towards the good, we implore You to let St. Raphael be our advisor in matters of the heart. Open our eyes to recognize the signs You bestow upon us and our ears to hear the gentle whisper of Your voice in our lives.

Bless our hearts with patience and hope, that we may wait upon Your perfect timing and not succumb to the snares of this fleeting world. Let our desire for companionship not lead us to paths divergent from Your righteousness, but instead draw us closer to You.

St. Raphael the Archangel, advocate of matrimonial unity, we venerate you this day and implore you to present our supplications before the throne of God. Through your intercession, may our lives be enriched with the blessings of a holy and loving partnership.

We conclude today's novena with a hope-filled heart, confident in the belief that St. Raphael is accompanying us and interceding for our earnest petitions.

In the name of the Father, and of the Son, and of the Holy Spirit. Amen.

Fifth Day

Beloved St. Raphael, blessed guide of the solitary heart, we enter the fifth day of our novena with hearts uplifted in hope and eyes set upon the horizon of holy love. Today, we seek your intercession for joyful and meaningful encounters. You are the patron of happy meetings, and thus, we implore your guidance to lead us towards such divine appointments, where our paths may cross with the one whom God has preordained for us.

In the scriptures, you, O St. Raphael, facilitated the meeting of Tobias and Sarah, turning their sorrow into joy, their solitude into companionship. We ask now for the wisdom to discern and the grace to appreciate the significance of moments and connections that define the tapestry of our lives. Just as each thread has its purpose in the weave, so may each encounter have its place in Your grand design for our future.

May our interactions with others be colored with the richness of divine love and purpose. Let each conversation, each shared laugh, each exchanged glance, carry the potential of revealing Your plans for us. Teach us to treat all individuals who cross our path with respect and kindness, so that through these virtues, we may attract the soul destined to walk beside us.

We pray fervently that our encounters will be free of superficiality and full of the depth that comes from You, Who are Love itself. May our meetings be marked not by the fleeting desires of earthly whims but by the profound connection that resonates with the melody of Eternal Love. In each interaction, grant us the discernment to see beyond the veil of appearances and to touch the true soul beneath, seeking in each heart a reflection of Your Divine Image.

If, in Your wisdom, we are to meet our future spouse today

or in days to come, ready our hearts for this joyous revelation. Let not anxiety or impatience taint our hopeful anticipation of love's blossoming. Instead, bless us with patience and a joyful spirit that takes delight in the unfolding of Your sacred plan. Shape us into beacons of faith and love, so that when we do meet our future spouse, we are worthy of them as they are of us.

St. Raphael, we also seek the strength to persist in our faith journey should our desired meetings be delayed. May we not falter or fall into despair but instead embrace each day as a step closer to our divine appointment. Make us instruments of your peace and joy, that even as we search for our companion, we might create happy encounters for others through our words, deeds, and prayers.

We surrender our longing for human companionship to the most sacred Heart of Jesus, through your holy intercession, St. Raphael. May the Divine Lover of all souls grant us the miracle of love in His perfect time, and may joyful encounters lead us along His path to the one who is meant to be our closest companion on this earthly pilgrimage toward Heaven.

Amen.

Sixth Day

Let us begin with the sign of our faith. In the name of the Father, and of the Son, and of the Holy Spirit. Amen.

Dear brothers and sisters in faith, today we find solace in the mighty deeds of our blessed companion in the journey, St. Raphael the Archangel. As we embark on the sixth day of this sacred novena, let us meditatively place ourselves in the presence of God, seeking the powerful aid of St. Raphael in surmounting the diverse hurdles that may beset our path to true love and companionship.

Reflecting on the holy scriptures, we remember the noble tale of Tobit and his beloved son Tobias. Within this story, a virtuous woman named Sarah was entwined in the heartrending predicament of marriage thwarted by a malevolent spirit. Bound by an affliction that repelled the blessing of marital bliss, Sarah's plight reminds us of the unforeseen trials that we, too, might encounter in our aspirations for a holy union.

In earnest prayer, let us humbly implore St. Raphael, who intervened so effectively in Sarah's life, to intercede for us, that any spiritual, emotional, or worldly barriers to our godly matrimony might be dispelled. In the celestial grace and wisdom of our Almighty Father, may we find the fortitude to confront and conquer that which seeks to separate us from our heart's true call to love as God loves.

Holy Archangel Raphael, traveler and comforter to those on the perilous road of life, you know the pangs of solitude and the quiet desperation that can dwell within the hearts of those yearning for their life's companion. Look kindly upon our desires for partnership, and plead our cause before the Throne of God. Bring to light the obstructions that lie hidden, and provide us with the divine strength to forge through the shadows of doubt and the chains of past afflictions.

We pray for clarity to discern the inclinations that may lead us astray, and the valor to correct our course with the guidance of the Holy Spirit. We ask for the grace to embrace the sanctity of patience, for in the rush to find love, we must not hasten past the wisdom found in waiting upon the Lord.

Dear St. Raphael, just as you revealed the path to Tobias and bound the forces that opposed the fulfillment of matrimonial joy for Sarah, we beseech you to protect us from the snares of the evil one and from the pitfalls intrinsic to our human frailty.

May the love we seek reflect the purity and constancy of the Holy Family, and through your esteemed intercession, may we be ever more prepared to receive the gift of a devoted soulmate, bestowed by our loving Creator.

Join me now in praying the prayer specific to the sixth day of our novena.

(Prayer for the Sixth Day)

St. Raphael, you were sent by God to assist Sarah and bring healing to her afflictions. In like manner, assist us, we pray, on our journey towards matrimonial unity. Cast away the obstacles that impede our pursuit of a holy partnership, and heal us from the wounds of our past, that we may be purified in heart, soul, and mind for the love that God ordains for us.

We entrust this novena, our hearts, and our future into your cherubic hands. Through your guidance, may we find a love that leads to the ultimate union with Christ.

St. Raphael, beloved Archangel, intercede for us in this novena of love as we say,

Hail Mary, full of grace, the Lord is with thee; blessed art thou amongst women and blessed is the fruit of thy womb, Jesus. Amen.

Seventh Day

Beloved St. Raphael, guide of those seeking companionship and love, on this seventh day of our novena, we approach you with hearts yearning for a love that echoes the divine. We recall the pure and chaste union of Tobiah and Sarah, a relationship you nurtured under the gazes of Heaven, untainted by the shadows of this world.

We live in a time where values seem shifting, where love's sacredness is often forgotten, and where purity is tested. Yet, within the depths of our hearts, we know that a love born in purity is a fortress; it is a testament to the genuine reflection of God's love for us.

In this moment of intimate supplication, we place before you our wish for a soulmate, with whom we can share a bond as profound as that of Tobiah and Sarah. May our future relationship be rooted in mutual respect and aspire towards the chastity and beauty their love portrayed. We pray for protection from temptation and for the grace to remain steadfast in our commitment to a pure and loving relationship that glorifies God.

Heavenly St. Raphael, protector of those who pray for a righteous partner, shelter our hearts from the snares that threaten to corrupt our desire for a holy love. Encourage us to maintain our resolve, recognizing that the worth of our future love is magnified when sanctified by God's will and commandments. May our souls be as clear mirrors, reflecting integrity, trust, and a love that aspires to ascend to the divine.

Help us to understand that true love waits, that it is not hasty, and that it grows under the gentle light of patience and prayer. Teach us that the body is a temple of the Holy Spirit, and that in honoring this temple, we honor the creator Himself. In our search for love, may we never forget the dignity bestowed upon us, and may our union be a witness to the sacredness and nobility of choice.

As we entrust ourselves to your guidance, dear St. Raphael, we are reminded of the reverence with which you accompanied Tobiah, watching over his journey and ultimately leading him to Sarah. Lead us likewise through the complexities of finding a spouse in this modern age, and bringing us to a soulmate whose heart is aligned with ours, in the pursuit of a love that mirrors the holy union of two souls wholly devoted to God.

Guardian angel St. Raphael, wrap us in your loving care, so that one day, when we meet the one whom God prepared for us, we may together offer a testimony of love that is both a reflection of Heaven's grace and a beacon of hope to the world.

In your holy intercession, may we discover the strength and wisdom needed for this blessed pilgrimage toward a sanctified partnership, sown in virtue and harvested in eternal joy.

Let us pray.

(Insert the prayer intended for the specific day)

Amen.

Eighth Day

As we enter the eighth day of our sacred novena, we recognize the profound grace that has carried us thus far on our journey. We have reached this penultimate day with hearts full of gratitude, reflecting on the myriad blessings that have cascaded upon us. Our sincere thanks go to the Almighty, who in His infinite wisdom, has bestowed upon us the loving intercession of St. Raphael, the patron of happy encounters.

Today, let us pause and look back upon our lives. Even in moments of solitude and yearning, we have never truly been alone. The hand of God, gently guided by St. Raphael, has been ever-present. As we seek the soulmate whom God has deemed fit for us, we are grateful for the unwavering love and support that surrounds us, seen and unseen.

In the quiet of this day's prayer, we focus on the virtue of thankfulness. With serene hearts, we acknowledge each of life's blessings—the laughter, the love, the lessons learned. For in each experience, the divine is whispering to us, nurturing our growth so that when our paths cross with our future soulmate, we will be ready to welcome them with open arms and a spirit shaped by divine encounters.

In our gracious contemplation, we cannot overlook the potential challenges and tribulations that have strengthened our resolve. Each hardship faced with faith has been an opportunity to deepen our trust in the Lord's grand design. We remember that St. Raphael, in his Biblical journey with Tobias, provided not only companionship but also healing and protection. Let us be thankful for the struggles, for they have provided us with resilience and a closer connection to God.

As we offer thanks, let us also lift our hearts in a renewal of trust. We place our future and our desires into the hands of

God, confident that He, who is Love itself, desires our true happiness. May our faith in God's plan be as unwavering as the mountains, strengthened by the angelic guidance of St. Raphael.

In the spirit of gratitude, we pray:

O Glorious St. Raphael, whose name means "God heals," thank you for the healing you bring to our hearts and the guidance you offer on our path. Your presence in our lives has been a source of comfort and strength. As we draw closer to the end of this novena, we renew our commitment to trust in God's timing and divine providence.

Bless us, St. Raphael, with the grace of a grateful heart that we may recognize and cherish every sign of God's love in our daily walk. We acknowledge that each day is a gift, filled with the potential of divine encounters and the prospect of meeting the one with whom we can share a holy and loving union.

Heavenly Father, thank You for the joys and challenges that shape us. With St. Raphael as our advocate, we look forward to the fulfillment of Your promise of companionship and love. Amen.

Tomorrow, as we conclude our novena, let us prepare to receive the fullness of God's blessings with unwavering hope, knowing that in His time, all will be revealed, all will be granted according to His divine will and perfect love.

Ninth Day

Today marks the culmination of our sacred novena, a journey we embarked upon with faith-filled hearts and hopeful spirits. As we stand at the threshold of this final day, let us hold steadfast to the love and patience that we have fostered within ourselves, trusting in the guidance of St. Raphael, the healer, the guide, and the patron of happy encounters.

In prayerful reflection, we turn our thoughts to the courageous journey of Tobiah and Sarah, a divine testament to the power of trust in the Lord, and the miraculous intercession of St. Raphael. May we, too, find the courage to open our hearts to the soulmate that God has destined for us. When they cross our path, may we recognize them with clarity of spirit and the reassurance that comes from the prayers we have offered up to heaven.

Heavenly Father, in Your profound wisdom, You have designed each of our lives with intent and grace. Bestow upon us the courage to not be deterred by past setbacks or fears. As we reach the end of this novena, let it not be the end of our pursuit, but rather the strengthening of our resolve to love and be loved, to cherish the companion You have in mind for us.

Glorious St. Raphael, on this concluding day, we ask for your potent blessing upon our future union. May it be sanctified by God's will, a beacon of light that mirrors the holy bond shared by Tobiah and Sarah. Through your intercession, may our love story unfold with the joy and purity that comes from a relationship rooted in God's love.

We pray for wisdom—to care for this sacred bond with tenderness and resilience, to nurture our love with kindness and understanding, and to foster a partnership that reflects the teachings of Jesus Christ. Grant us, dear St. Raphael, the discernment to work through trials with patience and grace, to surrender our tribulations to the Lord, and to celebrate our triumphs with humble hearts.

As we anticipate the joyous encounter with our soulmate, let us not forget the essence of companionship. Our love is not merely an exchange of emotion, but a reflection of God's unfailing love for us—a tender, profound, and everlasting covenant. May this understanding guide us as we embrace our future together, preparing ourselves for a life of shared faith, mutual service, and collective journey towards divine fulfillment.

Dear Patron of Love and Marital Harmony, we entrust our fervent hopes and dreams into your celestial care. With your gentle touch, guide us towards the love that awaits, and bless this union with every beatitude that heaven bestows.

In closing, we offer up our gratitude for the comfort and companionship we have found in prayer over these nine days. May we come forth from this novena reaffirmed in spirit, and with hearts wide open to the love that is yet to come, under the watchful gaze of our Almighty Father, through Christ our Lord. Amen.

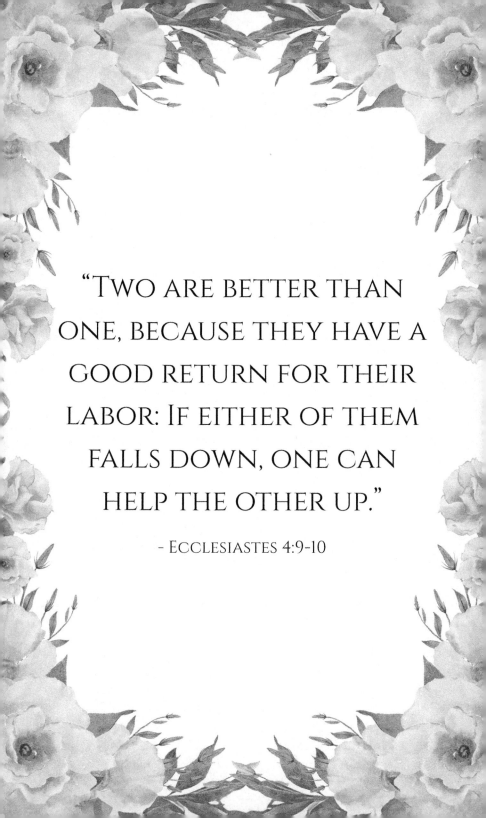

"Two are better than one, because they have a good return for their labor: If either of them falls down, one can help the other up."

- Ecclesiastes 4:9-10

Thank you!

We greatly value your feedback on this book and invite you to share your thoughts directly with us. As a growing independent publishing company, we continuously aim to improve the quality of our publications.

For your convenience, the QR code below will lead you to our website. There, you can leave feedback directly to us or find the link to the Amazon review page to share your experience and offer any suggestions for improvement. On our website, you can also view our related books and access free supplementary materials.

Related books

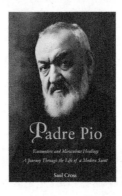

Printed in Great Britain
by Amazon

39798077R00056